There Was an Ol' Cajun

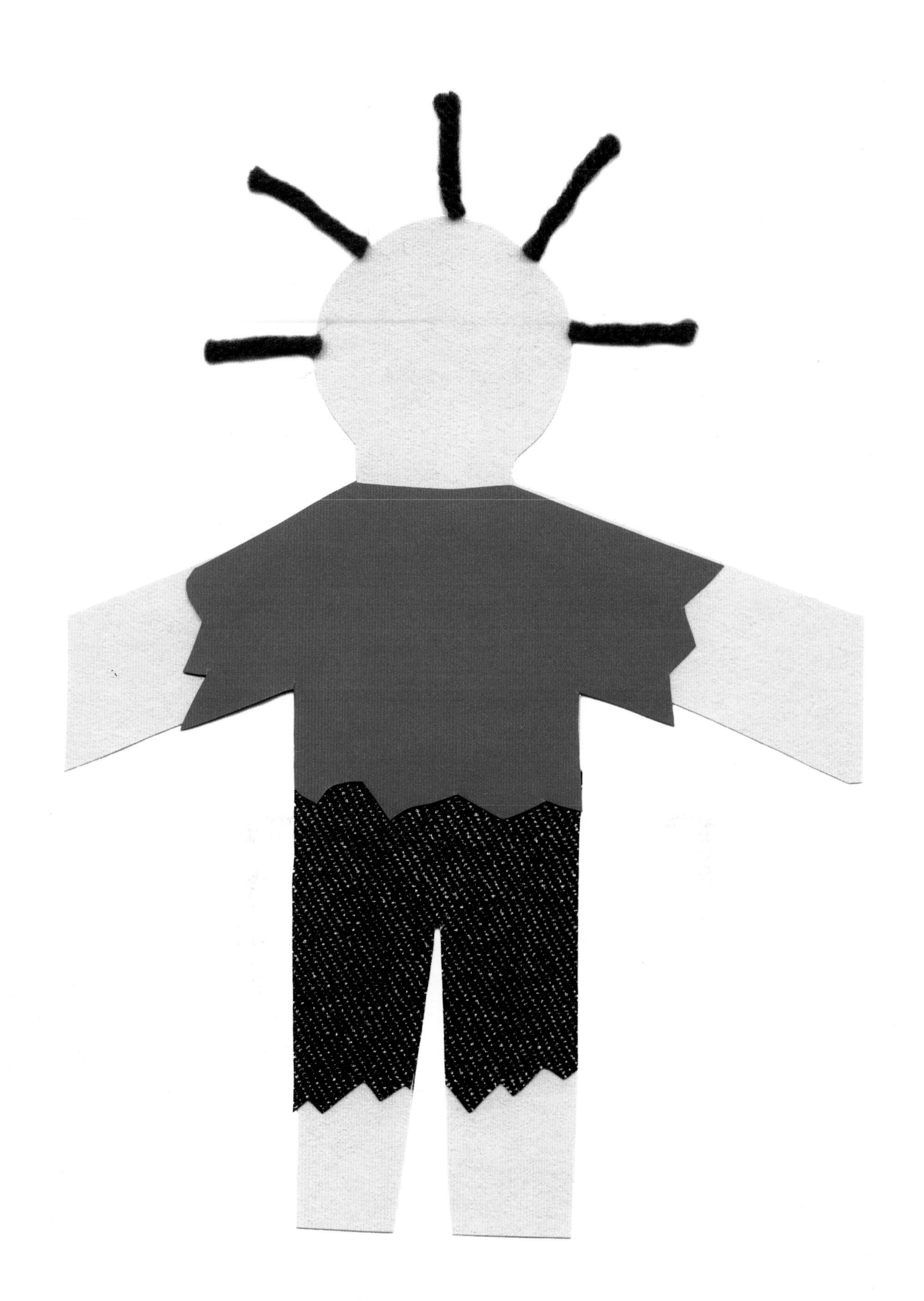

There Was an Ol' Cajun

Written and Illustrated by
Deborah Ousley Kadair

Happy reading!! Deborah Kadair

PELICAN PUBLISHING COMPANY
Gretna 2002

For my three favorite ol' Cajuns,
Dad, Greg, and Alex

The word "Pelican" and the depiction of a pelican are trademarks of Pelican Publishing Company, Inc., and are registered in the U.S. Patent and Trademark Office.

Printed in Hong Kong

Published by Pelican Publishing Company, Inc.
1000 Burmaster Street, Gretna, Louisiana 70053

There Was an Ol' Cajun

There was an ol' Cajun who swallowed a gnat. Imagine that, he swallowed a gnat.

Why he did dat?

There was an ol' Cajun who swallowed a skeeter. That silly ol' geezer swallowed a skeeter. He swallowed the skeeter to eat the gnat. Imagine that, he swallowed a gnat.

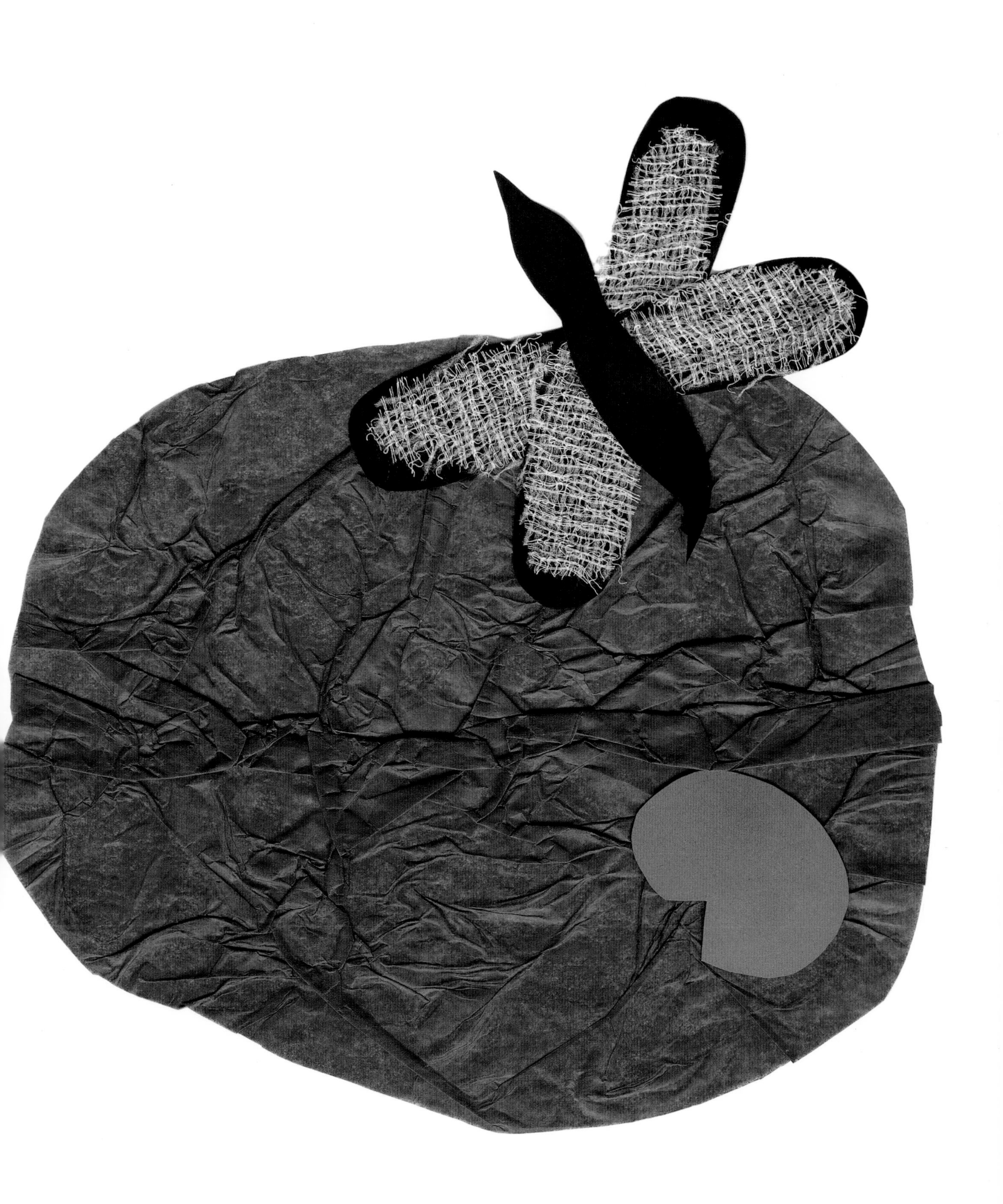

Why he did dat?

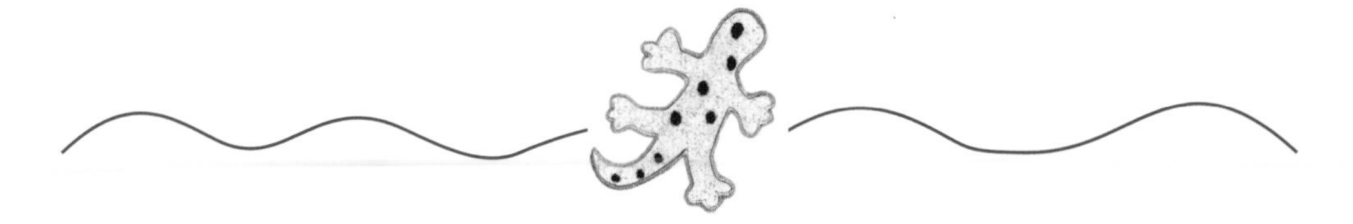

There was an ol' Cajun who swallowed a newt. That crazy coot swallowed a newt. He swallowed the newt to eat the skeeter. That silly ol' geezer swallowed a skeeter. He swallowed the skeeter to eat the gnat. Imagine that, he swallowed a gnat.

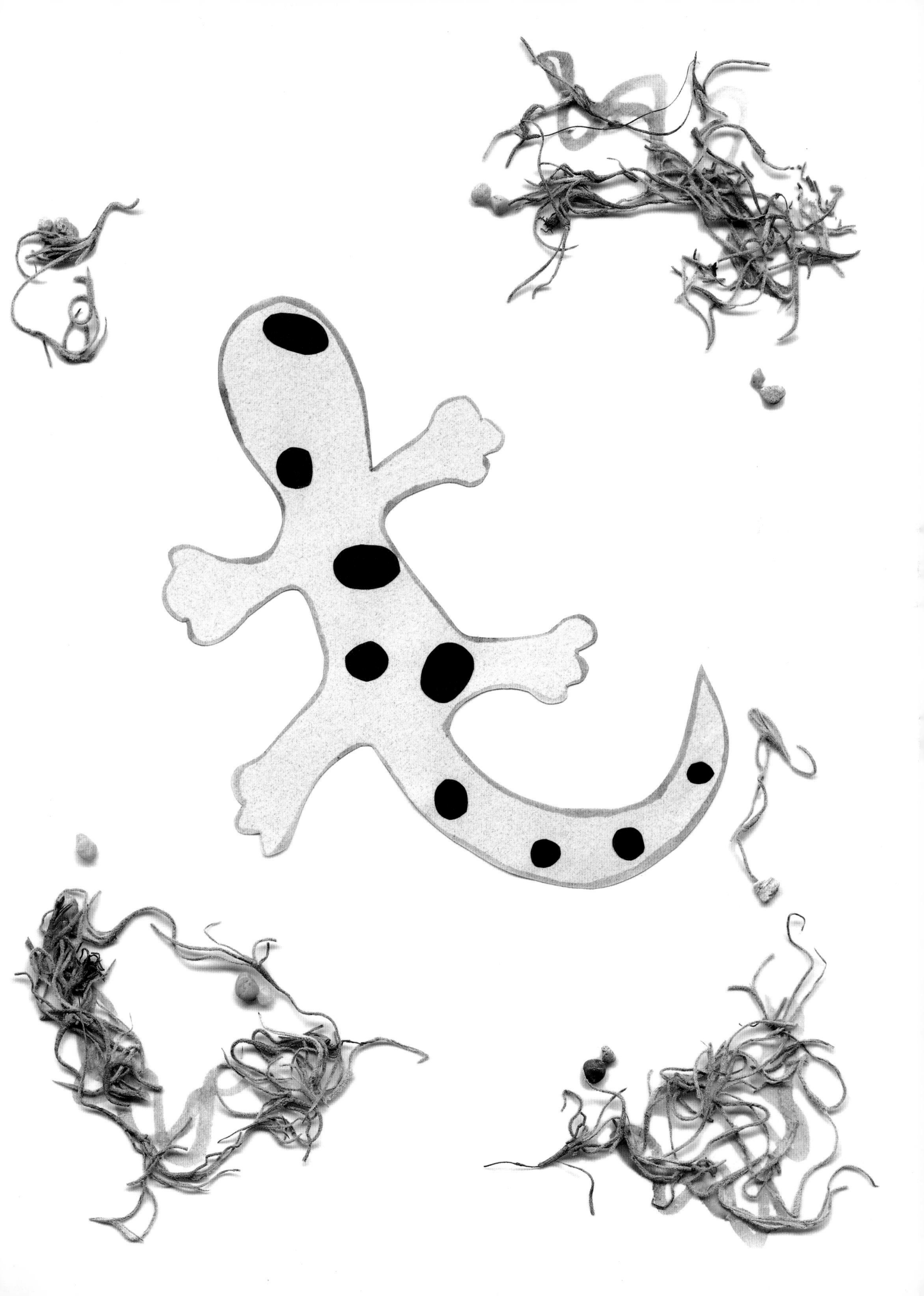

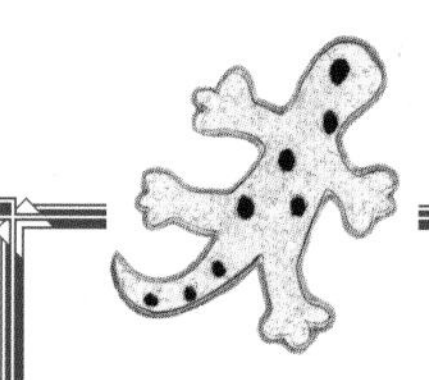

Why he did dat?

There was an ol' Cajun who swallowed a gar. He's gone too far, swallowing a gar. He swallowed the gar to eat the newt. That crazy coot swallowed a newt. He swallowed the newt to eat the skeeter. That silly ol' geezer swallowed a skeeter. He swallowed the skeeter to eat the gnat. Imagine that, he swallowed a gnat.

Why he did dat?

There was an ol' Cajun who swallowed a coon. What a bafoon, to swallow a coon. He swallowed the coon to eat the gar. He's gone too far, swallowing a gar. He swallowed the gar to eat the newt. That crazy coot swallowed a newt. He swallowed the newt to eat the skeeter. That silly ol' geezer swallowed a skeeter. He swallowed the skeeter to eat the gnat. Imagine that, he swallowed a gnat.

Why he did dat?

There was an ol' Cajun who swallowed a hound. He's big and round since he swallowed a hound. He swallowed the hound to get the coon. What a bafoon, to swallow a coon. He swallowed the coon to eat the gar. He's gone too far, swallowing a gar. He swallowed the gar to eat the newt. That crazy coot swallowed a newt. He swallowed the newt to eat the skeeter. That silly ol' geezer swallowed a skeeter. He swallowed the skeeter to eat the gnat. Imagine that, he swallowed a gnat.

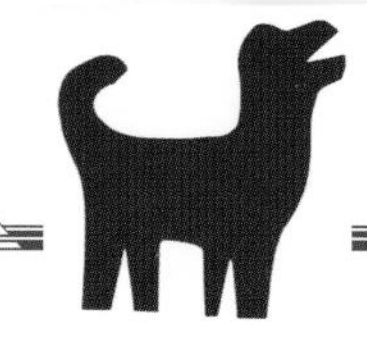

Why he did dat?

There was an ol' Cajun who, not too much later, went to the bayou and swallowed a gator! He swallowed the gator to eat the hound. He's big and round since he swallowed a hound. He swallowed the hound to get the coon. What a bafoon, to swallow a coon. He swallowed the coon to eat the gar. He's gone too far, swallowing a gar. He swallowed the gar to eat the newt. That crazy coot swallowed a newt. He swallowed the newt to eat the skeeter. That silly ol' geezer swallowed a skeeter. He swallowed the skeeter to eat the gnat. Imagine that, he swallowed a gnat. **Why he did dat?**

So he opened wide and . . . **GULP!**

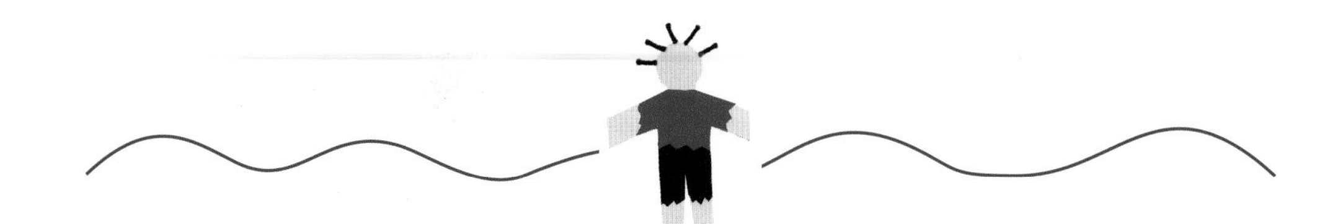

There was an ol' gator who swallowed a Cajun. He must be brazen, to swallow a Cajun.

Why he did dat?